MW01122649

Animal Encounters

A CHAPTER BOOK

Atif Toor

children's press®
A Division of Scholastic Inc.
New York   Toronto   London   Auckland   Sydney
Mexico City   New Delhi   Hong Kong
Danbury, Connecticut

For Leila and Olivia

ACKNOWLEDGMENTS

The author would like to thank everyone who gave their time and shared their knowledge to make this book possible. In particular, special thanks go to Tammy Renaud of the Texas Marine Mammal Stranding Network; Mary Liebau of Coast is Clear Farm and Kennels; Todd Malmsbury and Wendy Hanophy of the Colorado Division of Wildlife; Stephen Alter; and S. S. Bist, Director, Project Elephant. In addition, the author would like to thank Cathy Nichols, Iram Khandwala, Jigna Dodhia, Linda Falken, and Kirsten Hall for all their hard work and helpful advice.

Library of Congress Cataloging-in-Publication Data

Toor, Atif, 1971-
Animal encounters : a chapter book / by Atif Toor.
   p. cm. — (True tales)
Includes bibliographical references and index.
ISBN 0-516-25190-2 (lib. bdg.)   0-516-25455-3 (pbk.)
1. Human-animal relationships—Juvenile literature. I. Title. II. Series.
   QL85.T66 2005
   590—dc22
                     2005004779

CONTENTS

INTRODUCTION

When people and animals meet, anything can happen. Sometimes these **encounters** are happy ones. Christopher Cruse was walking on a beach when he discovered and then helped rescue a dolphin. Mary Liebau adopted and trained several border collies to help keep a local park clear of Canada geese.

Sometimes, though, encounters between animals and people can be dangerous. Linda Walters had no idea that she would be threatened by a mountain lion when she went for a jog on a beautiful June day. Caretaker Vijayan never expected to be lifted and tossed to the ground by an elephant under his watch.

Turn the page to learn more about how a man saved a friendly dolphin, a gaggle of geese was sent packing, a runner escaped the clutches of hungry mountain lions, and some elephants were given a second chance at happiness.

CHAPTER ONE

RESCUING CUPID

On February 14, 2004, a fisherman named Christopher Cruse was walking along Bryan Beach in Texas. He spotted something washed up on the shore. When he came closer, he saw it was a young dolphin. At first the animal wasn't moving. Then its tail flapped slightly. The dolphin needed help.

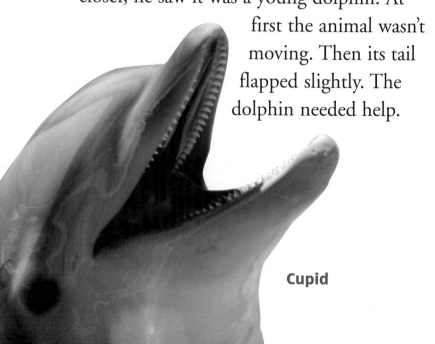

Cupid

Cupid was stranded on a Texas beach and needed help.

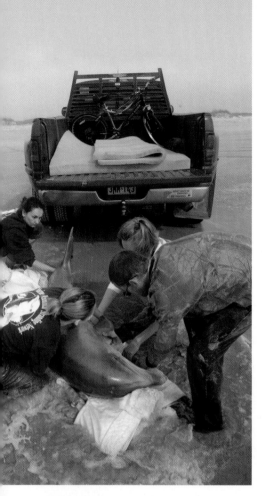

Volunteers lift Cupid onto a stretcher before putting him onto a truck.

Christopher alerted the Texas Marine Mammal Stranding Network (TMMSN). The people at the Stranding Network are experts in saving animals like dolphins, whales, and sea lions.

Tammy Renaud arrived on the beach with other **staff** members. They had to get the dolphin to the Stranding Network quickly, because he could not live out of the water for very long. They carefully put the dolphin on a stretcher and loaded him onto a truck. They kept him wet during the one-hour drive by pouring water over his body.

When the dolphin arrived at the Stranding Network, he was lowered into a special pool. He was weak, and weighed only 185 pounds (84 kilograms). A dolphin his age should weigh about 240 pounds (109 kilograms). His caregivers prepared food made of ground-up fish and baby formula to help him gain strength and weight. After a few days, the dolphin was strong enough to eat whole fish.

The staff named their new guest Cupid because he was found on Valentine's Day. As Cupid grew stronger, it became clear that he loved being around people and playing games.

Dolphins are very intelligent animals. They are easily bored in **captivity**. To keep Cupid entertained, Tammy gave him toys. She would hide a fish in one of his toys so he would have to search for his snacks.

Cupid plays with one of his toys.

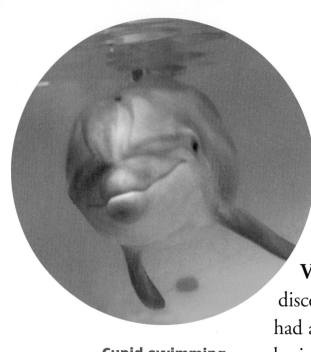
Cupid swimming

Sometimes, Cupid became confused. His body would stiffen and he would swim in small circles. **Veterinarians** discovered that he had a problem in his brain that caused him to have seizures. There was no cure for Cupid's problem. He could still lead a long, healthy life, but he could not go back to the ocean. Cupid risked being attacked by sharks and killer whales if he were to have a seizure in the open water.

After spending almost a year at the Stranding Network, Cupid needed a **permanent** home. Tammy and the Stranding Network staff chose Six Flags Marine World in Vallejo, California. There would be plenty of room for Cupid at Marine World. Even better, other dolphins lived there, so Cupid would have company.

Now the challenge was getting Cupid to his new home. Tammy called Federal Express, a shipping company. She knew Federal Express delivered **cargo** all over the world. Would they be able to **transport** a 230-pound (104-kilogram) dolphin?

Cupid had to travel from Galveston, Texas, to Vallejo, California, a distance of almost 2,000 miles (3,219 kilometers).

The people at Federal Express agreed to take Cupid to his new home free of charge. They would fly Cupid to California on a cargo plane in a special container filled with water. To prepare for his long journey, Cupid had to get used to the container. Cupid's caregivers put him in the container for twenty minutes at a time. Each time he was placed in the container, he was rewarded with food. Soon, Cupid was in the container for an hour at a time.

Cupid being placed in his special container

Cupid in his container on the plane

On the day of Cupid's big move, a team of sixteen people was on duty to take him to the airport. Members of the transport team lifted Cupid into his container and then loaded him onto a truck. Other members loaded him onto the plane. Tammy and a veterinarian stayed with Cupid during the long flight.

When he arrived at Marine World, Cupid was kept in a pool by himself so he could get used to his surroundings. Tammy stayed nearby for a few days to make sure Cupid didn't have any problems in his new **environment**.

After thirty days, Cupid's new caregivers introduced him to a dolphin named Brady. Cupid was placed in a pool. A gate separated him from Brady. The two dolphins looked at each other through the gate. When Brady was let into Cupid's pool, the dolphins immediately started touching and playing together.

Today, Cupid is a full-grown dolphin. He has a very active social life with the other dolphins at Marine World.

Cupid with one of his caregivers at Marine World

CHAPTER TWO

A WILD GOOSE CHASE

Splash! Mazy dives into the water at the Boston Public Garden. She swims towards a flock of Canada geese gathered in the middle of the pond. The frightened geese honk and fly away to escape the approaching dog. Mazy is a four-year-old **border collie** trained by Mary Liebau.

Border collie

This border collie is chasing a Canada goose.

Mary Liebau with one of the border collies she trains

Mary has been training border collies to **herd** geese at public parks, ponds, and golf courses for the past six years. She uses her hands and voice to teach them different commands. Border collies are known for their intelligence and great skill at herding animals like sheep. Why, though, would a dog need to herd wild Canada geese?

In the early 1900s, the Canada goose population was on the **decline**. Hunting and loss of **habitat** were to blame. Fortunately, laws were passed to protect the geese, and their numbers increased. Thanks to hunting restrictions and more protected breeding areas, there are now more Canada geese in North America than ever before.

Public parks, ponds, and golf courses make good homes for Canada geese. The geese feed on the grasses and build nests near the water. They have no **predators** to worry about in public areas, and they aren't easily frightened by humans. Many people feed Canada geese, making the birds even more comfortable around humans.

Canada geese aren't always good neighbors, however. When too many Canada geese feed on a lawn, they can damage the grass. An adult Canada goose can produce up to 1.5 pounds (680 grams)

This border collie goes into lakes and ponds to herd the geese.

A Canada goose guards its nest

of droppings per day. If a flock of 500 geese settle in at a park or golf course, workers have to clean up as much as 750 pounds (340 kilograms) of goose droppings per day!

During breeding season, Canada geese become very **aggressive**. If you happen to walk too close to a nest—watch out. The male goose, also known as a gander, guards the nest. If he feels his young are in danger, he will hiss, flap his wings, and snap at the **intruder**.

Because of these problems, people started looking for ways to get the geese out of parks and golf courses. Park superintendents

put up flags, tied aluminum pie plates on strings, and put out scarecrows to scare geese away. One golf course in Massachusetts even had two golfers run up and down the **fairways** each day, barking like dogs.

In 1992, Richard Marcks, a park superintendent at a country club in Greenwich, Connecticut, became fed up with the Canada geese that were making a mess of the club grounds. He remembered watching border collies herd cattle when he was younger. "I got in touch with the American Border Collie Association, and when I told them what I wanted the dogs for, they thought I was crazy," Richard said. Still, he contacted a border collie breeder

These dogs are being trained to herd.

who sold him a two-year-old dog named Tac. Richard learned different herding commands and used them to train Tac at the country club. Tac did such a great job scaring the geese away that Richard decided to train other border collies. Eventually, Richard started a company called "Geese Police." It sends geese-herding border collies to parks, golf courses, cemeteries, and playgrounds around the country.

In the past few years, more and more people are using border collies to solve their Canada goose problem. Mary Liebau started her service with a dog named Bucket. Now she works with twelve dogs. Many of them, like Mazy, were rescued from animal shelters. The dogs have lots of energy and can chase geese for hours each day. Since border collies are herding dogs, they follow commands and don't hurt the animals they chase. After several weeks of being chased, the geese usually get the hint that they aren't welcome. Soon, they fly away and find another place to settle—one where they won't be disturbed.

Mary Liebau with four of her twelve dogs

CHAPTER THREE

MOUNTAIN LIONS ON THE PROWL

In 1990, twenty-eight-year-old Linda Walters was jogging in Four Mile Canyon, Colorado. The sun was setting on a beautiful summer day in June when two mountain lions approached her. Linda shouted and waved her arms at them, trying to scare them off. It didn't work. The two animals came nearer.

The mountain lion is a member of the cat family.

Linda climbed up a nearby tree, but the mountain lions climbed up after her. One even scratched the back of her leg with its sharp claws. It was only when Linda kicked at one animal with her foot and hit the other on the head with a branch that the animals climbed back down and left her alone.

Linda was lucky. Not every encounter with a mountain lion ends this way. Sometimes a person is injured or even dies from a mountain lion attack. Even so, mountain lions rarely go after humans. Only a handful of attacks are reported in the United States each year. In fact, mountain lions usually avoid people. They prefer hunting deer, elk, porcupines, rabbits, and other small animals.

In the past thirty years, the number of encounters between mountain lions and people has increased. In western parts of the United States, people are finding mountain lions not just in national parks and wilderness areas, but in city suburbs, too. In Boulder, Colorado, people have spotted mountain lions in their backyards.

As more people are living and exploring mountain-lion country, the chances of encounters with mountain lions are increasing. More and more houses are being built in places that were once considered mountain-lion habitats. Cities like Boulder and Denver are expanding. Hiking, camping, and outdoor activities in national parks have become more popular in recent years.

Todd Malmsbury works for the Colorado Division of Wildlife. He helps people learn about mountain lions. The Division of Wildlife creates booklets, newspaper ads, and television programs. They educate people about such wild-animal neighbors as deer, coyotes, black bears, and mountain lions. Todd hopes this information will teach people how to act if they encounter a wild animal, as well as how to keep these animals away from places where people live.

One reason mountain lions are showing up in city suburbs is that they are following deer. People plant trees and shrubs around their homes that attract deer. As more deer arrive to feed,

Todd Malmsbury

As cities and suburbs expand, people are coming into more direct contact with wildlife.

mountain lions follow. The mountain lions may also hunt pet dogs and cats they find around people's homes.

One of the best ways to stop mountain lions from going where people live is to keep their **prey** (PRAY) away. Mountain lions will stay out of city suburbs if they are unable to find food there. The Division of Wildlife lets people know about trees and shrubs they can plant that won't attract deer. People are told

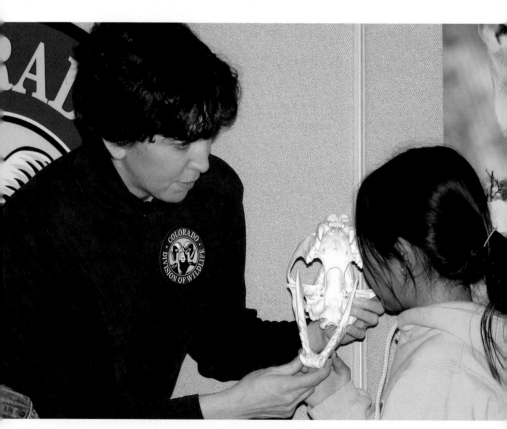

to keep their pets indoors. They are also told not to leave garbage out. Garbage attracts small animals such as raccoons, which mountain lions hunt.

Wendy Hanophy is an education specialist for the Colorado Division of Wildlife. She works with volunteers who visit schools to educate students and teachers about mountain

Wendy Hanophy, from the Colorado Division of Wildlife, is showing a student the skull of a mountain lion.

These wildlife managers are tagging a mountain lion. Tagging helps the managers keep track of the mountain lion's whereabouts.

lions. Students learn about how powerful mountain lions are, where they live, and what animals they hunt. Students learn never to approach or feed any wild animals and to avoid hiking alone in mountain-lion country.

Wildlife managers also try to train mountain lions to avoid people. The wildlife managers fire rubber pellets and use loud horns to frighten mountain lions that are spotted near hiking trails. They hope that this will keep mountain lions away from these trails.

Campers listen to a wildlife manager's safety advice.

Now that there are more people living in mountain-lion country, the chances of encounters between people and the big cats are greater than ever before. Through the efforts of public education programs, people and mountain lions will be able to share the land more safely.

CHAPTER FOUR

ELEPHANT CAMP

The panicked crowd pushed through the open gate of the **temple** in Tamil Nadu, India. Thayal Nayaki, an elephant that had lived most of her life on the temple grounds, had suddenly turned wild. The excited elephant lifted her caretaker, Vijayan, with her powerful trunk and tossed him to the ground. A team of veterinarians arrived at the scene and gave the elephant medicine to calm her down. Luckily, no one was seriously hurt. After a few hours of rest, Thayal Nayaki was back to normal.

Asian temple elephant

In India, decorated elephants are used in religious
ceremonies and festivals.

This work of art was painted by an Indian artist in the 17th century. It shows a nobleman riding an elephant.

For thousands of years, Indians captured wild elephants and kept them in temples. They trained them to haul trees and carry heavy loads. Kings often rode on elephants decorated in fabric and jewels. Military leaders used elephants to carry soldiers into battles. These days, bulldozers and trucks do much of the work elephants once did. However, some elephants still clear forests and haul logs because they can get to places where big vehicles cannot.

Although most Indian elephants live in the wild, thousands of working elephants

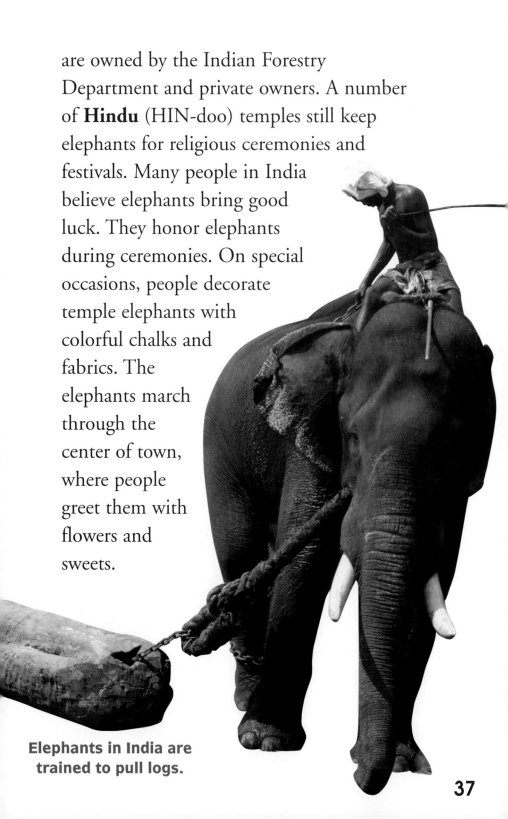

are owned by the Indian Forestry
Department and private owners. A number
of **Hindu** (HIN-doo) temples still keep
elephants for religious ceremonies and
festivals. Many people in India
believe elephants bring good
luck. They honor elephants
during ceremonies. On special
occasions, people decorate
temple elephants with
colorful chalks and
fabrics. The
elephants march
through the
center of town,
where people
greet them with
flowers and
sweets.

**Elephants in India are
trained to pull logs.**

37

Violent encounters between humans and working elephants can happen for many reasons. Temple elephants like Thayal Nayaki often live in cramped spaces. They are chained for several hours a day and can't roam freely as they would in the wild. Being surrounded by people can also cause stress in a weary elephant. Loud noises and sudden movements can frighten an elephant, sending it into a panic. Since an adult elephant can weigh up to 11,000 pounds (4,990 kilograms), an angry or frightened animal can cause a lot of damage.

It can be stressful for an elephant to be constantly surrounded by large groups of people.

A mahout rides an elephant.

Elephants living in captivity require lots of care and attention. In India, an elephant caretaker is called a **mahout** (ma-HOOT). Mahouts share a close bond with their elephants. They are responsible for training, feeding, and bathing their elephants. They also help their elephants stay healthy and treat them when they are ill. Working with

Mahouts take good care of their elephants.

elephants all day can be dangerous work. Elephants can be moody and sensitive. Some mahouts are attacked because they lack the proper skills to care for their elephants. Some mistreat the animals.

The government in the state of Tamil Nadu wanted to do something to reduce the number of elephant attacks and to improve the health of working elephants. The government ordered all working elephants in the state to be sent to a camp. There, for forty-five days, they could relax, roam freely, and receive medical care.

The Mudumalai Wildlife **Sanctuary** was selected for the campsite. The sanctuary is on a river with plenty of water for bathing and drinking. Workers built fences, and guards kept the visiting elephants safe from **poachers**.

Many elephants would have to be transported by truck over long distances to the sanctuary. Some people felt this would be dangerous and unhealthy for the elephants. Other people complained that the camp was an unecessary expense. Even so, the state government moved forward with the elephant camp.

On November 15, 2003, fifty-five elephants and their mahouts arrived at the camp. Every morning, each elephant was treated to a coconut oil massage. The elephants were fed fresh grasses twice a day, along with a special food made of rice, grains, herbs, and vitamins.

A mahout prepares a meal for the elephants.

Veterinarians gave the elephants check-ups and treated the ones that showed signs of illness. Mahouts attended training sessions to improve their skills in caring for elephants. The elephants enjoyed regular baths in the river. In the evenings, the elephants took long walks for exercise.

After their stay, the elephants were loaded back on the trucks and driven home. While some people still question the benefits of the elephant camp, many of the caretakers noted that their elephants' mood and health had improved. The government has declared that the elephant camp will be an **annual** event. Next year, many working elephants of Tamil Nadu will return to the Mudumalai Wildlife Sanctuary for more check-ups, relaxation, and river baths.

This elephant enjoys a bath at the camp.

GLOSSARY

aggressive ready to threaten or fight others

annual yearly

border collie a type of black-and-white dog that herds sheep and other animals

captivity the situation in which an animal has been taken out of its natural habitat and is being cared for in a place controlled by humans

cargo goods carried by an airplane, ship, or automobile

decline to get smaller

encounter an unexpected meeting

environment all the living things and conditions of a place

fairway the part of a golf course between the tee and the green on each hole

habitat the environment where an animal or plant naturally lives and grows

herd to make animals move as a group

Hindu (HIN-doo) having to do with Hinduism, a religion in India

intruder someone who goes into a place without being invited

mahout (ma-HOOT) someone who rides and cares for elephants

permanent lasting

poacher a person who illegally hunts animals protected by law

predator an animal that kills and eats other animals

prey (PRAY) an animal that is hunted by another animal for food

sanctuary a place in nature where animals are protected

staff a group of people who work for the same company or organization

temple a building where people worship

transport to move something from one place to another

veterinarian a doctor who treats animals

FIND OUT MORE

Rescuing Cupid
www.tmmsn.org/index.html
Learn more about how the Texas Marine Mammal
Stranding Network rescues and cares for dolphins and
other marine mammals.

A Wild Goose Chase
www.canadageese.org
Read what some people are doing to control Canada geese,
including using border collies.

Mountain Lions on the Prowl
www.dfg.ca.gov/lion
Hear a mountain lion roar and find out more about these
powerful predators.

Elephant Camp
www.forests.tn.nic.in/rejuvenation_camp.htm
Visit an elephant camp in India.

More Books to Read

Dolphin Adventure: A True Story by Wayne Grover and Jim
Fowler, HarperCollins, 2000

In the Forests with the Elephants by Roland Smith and
Michael J. Schmidt, Sagebrush Education Resources, 1998

Tooth and Claw: Animal Adventures in the Wild by Ted
Lewin, HarperCollins, 2003

*Working Like a Dog: The Story of Working Dogs through
History* by Gena K. Gorrell, Tundra Books, 2003

INDEX

PHOTO CREDITS

MEET THE AUTHOR

Atif Toor was born in Tarbela, Pakistan. He has worked as a writer, art director, and illustrator in children's publishing for the past ten years. Atif enjoys traveling around the world and had his own peaceful encounter with a herd of wild elephants while visiting a wildlife sanctuary in southern India. Atif currently lives in New York City, where his encounters with animals are usually limited to poodles, pigeons, and squirrels.